# The Concise Illustrated Book of
# **Roses**

## Beatrix Hamilton

*Grange*
BOOKS

Published in 1993
by Grange Books
An imprint of Grange Books Limited
The Grange
Grange Yard
London SE1 3AG

ISBN 1 85627 397 0

Printed in Singapore

*Acknowledgments*
All photographs from Images Colour Library
except for the following: Harry Smith
Collection 24, 25, 29, 39, 40, 45.

All artworks supplied by Maltings Partnership

*Page 7*: Peace.
*Right*: Handel (see page 37).

# CONTENTS

# Cultivating Roses

Roses prefer a sheltered, sunny spot and a well drained soil; but otherwise, these paragons are surprisingly easy going and will succeed in most gardens or backyards. In fact shrub roses will flourish on quite light, even poor soils.

## Preparing the soil

It is important to give your roses a really good start. This means some digging. So whether you are planning to plant a single rose or a large bed, it is advisable to double dig so the subsoil is well broken up, especially if drainage is less than perfect. Incorporate plenty of well-rotted garden compost or manure into the topsoil together with a sprinkling of bonemeal or general purpose, balanced fertilizer.

Always prepare the soil before your roses arrive, so, provided conditions are suitable, they can be planted straight away. If the soil is frozen or sodden, plants are best left in their wrappings in a cool, frost-free shed or garage until conditions improve enough for them to be heeled-in or planted.

## Planting

Bare-rooted plants ordered from a rose nursery will usually arrive early in winter as they must be lifted and replanted while still dormant. If the soil has been prepared and the ground is in a fit condition, they can be planted immediately. In fact, any time during the winter or even early in spring is suitable provided growth has not got underway. If the roots look at all dry, soak them in a bucket of water for 24 hours before planting.

Dig out a planting hole wide enough to accommodate the spread of the roots and deep enough just to cover the soil mark on the stem. Then, holding the rose in position, infill with soil, firming it round the roots with your hands as you go. The plant should sit just a little deeper than it did in its nursery bed.

Container-grown roses can be purchased and planted at any time of the year in theory. In practice, it is best to plant them in the autumn or early in spring. Apart from gently teasing out some of the outermost roots, do not disturb the rootball. In all other respects soil preparation and planting is the same as described above.

Never plant a rose on ground where other roses have been growing. They will rarely do well and will probably die. The soil seems to need a rest after supporting the queen of flowers.

## General care

In spring, check to see if frost has lifted the soil during the winter months and firm in your roses again if necessary. Spring is also the time for an annual mulch. Always apply this when the soil is moist. Use well rotted manure, garden compost, chipped bark or peat. This will not only conserve moisture and improve the condition of the soil, but also keep down the weeds. Roses are greedy feeders, so apply fertilizer after pruning in spring and again in summer just before flowering.

## Pruning

Bush roses (hybrid teas, floribundas and patio roses) are pruned each spring to keep them in shape and covered in flowers. (However any tall growth in danger of being snapped off by winter gales can be snipped back in late autumn.)

Using a pair of clean, sharp secateurs – the best you can afford – cut out completely any dead or damaged wood and weak spindly growth. Then remove any crossing branches and thin out the centre, if necessary, to keep it open. Cut back the remaining stems to about 30cm (1ft) in the case of floribundas. Prune hybrid teas more severely, down to about 20cm (8in), to encourage fewer but larger blooms. Always prune back to just above an outward-facing bud and angle the cut away from the bud. Miniature roses are pruned in much the same way but the healthy growths are lightly tipped back.

Climbing roses are best left unpruned for their first couple of years. They produce a framework of stems, bearing their flowers on later growths. In order to encourage new laterals to form the latter should be trimmed back to about three buds in spring.

Shrub roses need little in the way of regular pruning beyond cutting out any dead or weak stems. Thin out old growth from time to time and tip back tall unsightly stems as necessary.

Suckers can be a problem on any rose not growing on its own

roots. They arise from below the graft union and may be recognizable by their paler foliage. Scrape away the soil to expose the point of origin and, wearing a pair of thick gloves, pull the suckers off and replace the soil.

Deadheading is a form of summer pruning. It is important to carry this out regularly during the summer to keep up the production of flowers for as long as possible.

## Major pests and diseases

*Aphids (greenfly)* suck the sap causing distortion of young growth and foliage. Spray with pirimicarb or liquid derris at the first sign of an attack. A systemic insecticide will also do the job.

*Red spider mite* may be a problem in a dry summer, or on any rose growing under cover. The mites are barely visible and suck the sap causing leaves to yellow and fall. Try to keep the atmosphere moist and spray with fenitrothion if necessary.

*Caterpillars* can be picked off by hand. Use derris or permethrin if the outbreak is severe.

Three main diseases of roses are *black spot*, *mildew* and *rust*. *Black spot* appears on the leaves and if left untreated will cause them to yellow and fall. The plant will become weakened and suffer some degree of defoliation. Spray with benlate and make sure all affected foliage is collected up and disposed of, preferably by burning.

*Mildew* shows as a white powdery covering on young growth. Always collect and burn all affected prunings. Plant roses in an open position so that air can circulate freely around the plants. Spray susceptible varieties with benlate.

*Rust* can cause defoliation. Look out for rusty marks on the undersides of the leaves and spray with an appropriate chemical such as mancozeb.

# ALEC'S RED

**Country of origin:** Scotland
**Date:** 1970
**Raised by:** Cocker
**Type:** Hybrid tea (large-flowered bush rose)
**Colour:** Cherry red
**Height:** Approximately 75cm (2ft 6in)

**Description:** A wonderfully sweet-scented rose of upright habit, quite bushy with mid-green foliage. Each bloom is held on a strong growing stem. The flowers are abundant, and keep their colour well. Rounded in form, they open wide and flat. This rose is disease resistant.
**Special uses:** Suitable for exhibition, excellent for cutting. One of the best true reds. Leave about 50cm (20in) between plants in a bedding display.

**Description:** Probably the best of the 'blue' roses. It grows vigorously with glossy green foliage and large flowers. These are fragrant and well shaped, held on strong stems. Black spot can be a problem. Check the undersides of the leaves for tell-tale signs of rust.

**Special uses:** Much-loved by flower arrangers, this is a splendid rose for cutting, and is at its best when grown under glass.

**Synonym:** 'Mainzer Fastnacht', 'Sissi'
**Country of origin:** Germany
**Date:** 1964
**Raised by:** Tantau
**Type:** Hybrid tea (large-flowered bush rose)
**Colour:** Pale lilac-mauve
**Height:** Approximately 1m (3ft 3in)

# COLOUR WONDER

**Synonym:** 'Konigin der Rosen'
**Country of origin:** Germany
**Date:** 1964
**Raised by:** Kordes
**Type:** Hybrid tea (large-flowered bush rose)
**Colour:** Salmon, with pale yellow reverse
**Height:** Approximately 75cm (2ft 6in)

**Description:** An unusual hybrid tea rose with small, dark, glossy leaflets and lightly scented flowers of unusual colour and form. The reverses of the petals are paler and tinged with yellow. This rose is well worth looking out for.
**Special uses:** A most attractive rose for bedding. Keep in a bed on its own to get the best effect, spacing plants about 45cm (18in) apart. It is also suitable for planting in a container as long as the roots are not cramped.

**Description:** A bushy rose covered with dark green leaves. It has a long flowering period with blooms being produced throughout the summer and well into the autumn. These open quickly and are deliciously fragrant. However, the colour fades with age and the flowers suffer damage in wet weather, the petals balling and turning brown. Mildew can be a problem so it is advisable to plant this rose in an open position to ensure a free circulation of air. Even so routine spraying will usually be necessary.
**Special uses:** Good for bedding and as flowers for cutting.

**Synonym:** 'Herzog von Windsor'
**Country of origin:** Germany
**Date:** 1968
**Raised by:** Tantau
**Type:** Hybrid tea (large-flowered bush rose)
**Colour:** Vermilion
**Height:** Approximately 75cm (2ft 6in)

# GRANDPA DICKSON

**Synonym:** 'Irish Gold'
**Country of origin:** Ireland
**Date:** 1966
**Raised by:** Dickson
**Type:** Hybrid tea (large-flowered bush rose)
**Colour:** Yellow
**Height:** Approximately 1m (3ft 3in)

**Description:** The glossy deep green leaflets are small and rather sparsely produced on this bush of upright habit. The large, full blooms have some fragrance and pale attractively with age. Sometimes the petals are tinged with pink at the edges. This is a vigorous rose which has excellent resistance to disease provided the soil is kept in good condition.

**Special uses:** Good for exhibition and bedding. For the latter, space the bushes about 40cm (16in) apart. Suitable for growing under glass.

# HELEN TRAUBEL

**Description:** A vigorous rose with plentiful foliage. The young leaves have a pleasant copper tone turning dark green as they age. The flower colour may vary slightly. Nevertheless this is a beautiful rose, fragrant and with long pointed buds which eventually open wide. However, there is a tendency for the stems to droop at the neck which makes this rose unsuitable for cutting. 'Helen Traubel' stands up well to wet weather.

**Special uses:** Best used for bedding; about 50cm (20in) should be left between plants.

**Country of origin:** U.S.A.
**Date:** 1951
**Raised by:** Swim
**Type:** Hybrid tea (large-flowered bush rose)
**Colour:** Apricot
**Height:** Approximately 1m (3ft 3in)

# JUST JOEY

**Country of origin:** England
**Date:** 1973
**Raised by:** Cant
**Type:** Hybrid tea (large-flowered bush rose)
**Colour:** Copper
**Height:** Approximately 75cm (2ft 6in)

**Description:** One of the shorter growing hybrid teas. The young foliage is reddish and matures to deep green; the perfect foil to the distinctive flowers. These are large, slightly scented and copper coloured with petals ruffled at the edges. The blooms are held in small clusters or on single stems. The plant is resistant to disease and untroubled by rain.

**Special uses:** Good for bedding out as the flowering period is long and continues well into autumn. Leave about 45cm (18in) between plants. A strong necked rose excellent for cutting and much beloved by flower arrangers for its unique colour.

**Description:** This has attractive glossy green foliage. The 'Queen Elizabeth' in its parentage gives it a strong and upright growth as well as resistance to disease. The elegant blooms, although only slightly scented, are plentiful and produced on long thornless stems. This is quite the best white hybrid tea.

**Special uses:** Because of its upright habit of growth, it is suitable for an informal hedge. An excellent bedding rose which can also be grown as a standard. This is one of the best roses for cutting.

**Country of origin:** Belgium
**Date:** 1963
**Raised by:** Lens
**Type:** Hybrid tea (large-clustered bush rose)
**Colour:** White, almost cream in the centre
**Height:** Approximately 1m (3ft 3in)

# PEACE

**Synonyms:** 'Gioia', 'Gloria Dei', 'Mme A. Meilland'
**Country of origin:** France
**Date:** 1945
**Raised by:** Meilland
**Type:** Hybrid tea (large-flowered bush rose)
**Colour:** Pale yellow flushed with pink
**Height:** Up to 1.5m (5ft)

**Description:** One of the most famous and popular roses of all. It was given the name 'Peace' in the United States when its introduction happened to coincide with the fall of Berlin in the Second World War. It is a vigorous rose, growing tall and covered with glossy green foliage. The large flowers are particularly beautiful when fully open. The colour may vary slightly, and sometimes the pink tinge is absent; in any case it fades as the blooms mature. It has a long flowering period and its blooms are produced well into the autumn.

**Special uses:** It can be grown as a shrub or makes a most attractive hedge.

**Description:** This will form a tall upright bush with dark green, somewhat purplish foliage. The 'perfect' blooms are very large and heavy. Their colour is variable, ranging from bright pink shadings on a pale base to a more subtle combination of warm cream flushed pink at the edges of the petals.
**Special uses:** Good for cutting.

**Synonym:** 'Kordes' Perfecta'
**Country of origin:** Germany
**Date:** 1957
**Raised by:** Kordes
**Type:** Hybrid tea (large-flowered bush rose)
**Colour:** Cream shaded with deep pink
**Height:** Approximately 1m (3ft 3in)

17

# ROSE GAUJARD

**Country of origin:** France
**Date:** 1957
**Raised by:** Gaujard
**Type:** Hybrid tea (large-flowered cluster rose)
**Colour:** Carmine and white
**Height:** Approximately 1.2m (4ft)

**Description:** A vigorous and healthy rose with dark, glossy foliage. Slender flower buds open to display a brilliant bloom of silvery white strongly flushed with bright carmine on the insides of the petals. It is disease-resistant and very easy to grow.
**Special uses:** The strong colour is difficult to associate with other flowing plants, especially other roses. It is therefore advisable to plant 'Rose Gaujard' in a bed on its own or with a quiet background of foliage plants when it will form an eye-catching display. Leave about 60cm (2ft) between bushes.

**Description:** Vigorous, spreading and bushy, with dark green foliage, this rose grows well in most gardens. It is free-flowering and its richly coloured blooms are fragrant and well formed. It stands up well to wet weather and although usually untroubled by disease, look out for black spot. It is advisable to take routine measures at the first sign of this disease or if you know it to be a problem in your area.

**Special uses:** Suitable for exhibition. It can be trained to form a fine standard. One of the best for bedding – but on its own to make the most of the lovely warm colour. Bushes should be planted about 60cm (2ft) apart.

**Country of origin:** England
**Date:** 1959
**Raised by:** Gregory
**Type:** Hybrid tea (large-flowered bush rose)
**Colour:** Rosy red
**Height:** Approximately 90cm (3ft)

# CITY OF BELFAST

**Description:** The exceptionally brightly coloured blooms held in large sprays keep going all summer long. The young foliage is red, turning green as it matures. A disease resistant and reliable rose which is neat and bushy in habit.

**Special uses:** It will provide an eye-catching display when used as a bedding rose, a purpose for which its small stature is ideally suited. For maximum impact plant it in a bed on its own, with 40cm (16in) between plants.

**Country of origin:** Ireland
**Date:** 1968
**Raised by:** McGredy
**Type:** Floribunda (cluster-flowered bush rose)
**Colour:** Scarlet
**Height:** Approximately 60cm (2ft)

# ELIZABETH OF GLAMIS

**Description:** There are well-shaped double flowers held in small clusters. They are fragrant and turn pale as they open flat. To flourish, this rose needs a good deep well-drained soil and a sunny position – a heavy cold soil will probably prove deadly. Therefore incorporate plenty of well-rotted compost or manure when planting and mulch generously each spring as well as feeding it in summer. It needs a sheltered spot as it is not completely hardy and can be cut back by frost. Keep an eye open for signs of disease; its resistance is poor, especially to rust.

**Special features:** Of exceptional beauty if grown well, protected from the wind and generally indulged.

**Synonym:** 'Irish Beauty'
**Country of origin:** Ireland
**Date:** 1964
**Raised by:** McGredy
**Type:** Floribunda (cluster-flowered bush rose)
**Colour:** Salmon-pink
**Height:** 90cm (3ft) or more

# ENGLISH MISS

**Country of origin:** England
**Date:** 1979
**Raised by:** Cant
**Type:** Floribunda (cluster-flowered bush rose)
**Colour:** Light pink
**Height:** 75cm (2ft 6in)

**Description:** An attractive bush of medium height, it has a branching habit and young foliage of an attractive purple-green. The flowers are very freely produced and sweetly scented. They are rounded in form and can vary in colour from pale coral to almost white. Sometimes the petals appear edged with a deeper pink. This rose is disease-resistant despite its delicate appearance.
**Special uses:** It forms a good standard rose, and is one of the most beautiful pale pink roses for the garden or patio.

**Description:** 'Honeymoon' has large double flowers of clear yellow, and lovely pale green foliage, and is especially attractive when the leaves unfurl. Barely fragrant, this rose does best in cool climates. Bright sun and high temperatures adversely affect the flowering, colour and form of this otherwise easy-going floribunda.

**Special uses:** A hardy rose for exposed areas.

**Country of origin:** Germany
**Date:** 1959
**Raised by:** Kordes
**Type:** Floribunda (cluster-flowered bush rose)
**Colour:** Yellow
**Height:** Approximately 1m (3ft 3in)

# ICEBERG

**Synonyms:** 'Fée des Neiges', 'Schneewittchen'
**Country of origin:** Germany
**Date:** 1958
**Raised by:** Kordes
**Type:** Floribunda (cluster-flowered bush rose)
**Colour:** White
**Height:** Up to 1.5m (5ft)

**Description:** The best white floribunda of all and an outstanding rose in every respect. It has an attractive spreading habit and glossy green foliage. The pure white blooms, often tinged pink in bud, are double and open flat. These are lightly perfumed and held in large clusters. Wet weather seldom mars their appearance but mildew and black spot, especially, may be a problem. Routine measures may be necessary against the latter.

**Special uses:** As well as being a superb bedding rose – leave about 45cm (1ft 6in) between plants, 'Iceberg' can be more closely planted to form a hedge. It has stature enough to be used as a shrub in a mixed border.

# QUEEN ELIZABETH

**Description:** A favourite rose grown in many, many gardens and public places. Extremely vigorous with dark green, glossy foliage and stems which bear few thorns, this is an easy rose to grow and remarkably resistant to disease. The blooms are superb; fully double and of fine form, but with only a hint of fragrance. Sometimes they are borne on single stems, more often they occur in clusters. They stand up well to wet weather.

**Special uses:** Too tall for a bedding rose, 'Queen Elizabeth' is ideal in a mixed shrub border fronted by lower growing subjects. Close planted it will form a hedge, as it withstands hard pruning well. Long stems make this a good rose for cutting.

**Country of origin:** U.S.A.
**Date:** 1954
**Raised by:** Lammerts
**Type:** Grandiflora (U.S.A.) and floribunda (U.K.).
**Colour:** Pink
**Height:** 2m (6ft) or more

25

# SEA PEARL

**Synonym:** 'Flower Girl'
**Country of origin:** Ireland
**Date:** 1964
**Raised by:** Dickson
**Type:** Floribunda (cluster-flowered bush rose)
**Colour:** Orange and pink
**Height:** 1.2m (4ft) or more

**Description:** Rather tall, upright bush with vigorous growth. The foliage has a coppery tone. The colouring of the flowers is an unusual deep salmon pink with a peach reverse. However, it can vary in shade and depth. Slightly scented, the blooms are well shaped and stand up well to wet weather.

**Special uses:** This is best in a border or as a specimen with a background of green foliage to show off the flowers.

**Description:** A low growing rose, bushy in habit and very free flowering. The flowers are brilliantly coloured and held in dense clusters. Black spot may be a problem in some areas. It needs a sheltered position as it is not particularly hardy and may be damaged by frost.

**Special uses:** Plant on its own in a bed. Its small stature makes it ideal for the small garden. It is a good tub rose.

**Country of origin:** Germany
**Date:** 1972
**Raised by:** Tantau
**Type:** Floribunda (cluster-flowered bush rose)
**Colour:** Vermilion
**Height:** Approximately 60cm (2ft)

# YESTERDAY

**Country of origin:** England
**Date:** 1974
**Raised by:** Harkness
**Type:** Floribunda (cluster-flowered bush rose) or patio rose
**Colour:** Lilac-pink
**Height:** Up to 1m (3ft 3in)

**Description:** Although this rose is often grouped with the polyantha roses (forerunners of the floribundas) it has, in fact, none of their ancestry in its pedigree. However it does have many of their attributes. It forms a bushy shrub with tiny leaflets and numerous clusters of small, very sweet smelling flowers. These are semi-double and open in varying shades of lilac-pink. It is recurrent and reliable in bloom. Sometimes tall arching stems are produced and these will need to be cut back.

**Special uses:** Ideal as a specimen or standard rose. It can be planted towards the front of a mixed border. It is especially suitable for small gardens or for growing in a tub.

**Description:** It forms a small bushy shrub. The flowers are tiny double and vary somewhat in colour. They are usually a soft peachy pink but may be almost coral. Very healthy but not always completely hardy. All miniature roses grow on their own roots, so take half-ripe cuttings in summer, trim to 8cm (3in) and insert in sandy compost.

**Special uses:** Plant several of these little bushes in a window box or in a small tub and they will give a splendid show, flowering almost continuously from midsummer to mid-autumn. Suitable for exhibition. Grow under glass for indoor display.

**Country of origin:** U.S.A.
**Date:** 1964
**Raised by:** Moore
**Type:** Miniature
**Colour:** Peach
**Height:** Up to 30cm (1ft)

# DARLING FLAME

**Synonym:** 'Minuetto'
**Country of origin:** France
**Date:** 1971
**Raised by:** Meilland
**Type:** Miniature
**Colour:** Orange-vermilion
**Height:** Approximately 30cm (1ft)

**Description:** Brilliant flame-coloured flowers with gold reverse, double but without scent. They look outstanding massed together in a tub. Take half-ripe cuttings in midsummer to raise plenty of plants – one or two look lonely. With 'Zambra' in its parentage, black spot can be a problem.
**Special uses:** Best in small gardens or patios. Use to line a path or plant in a border with other shrubby subjects. They can look outstanding massed in a tub or container.

# MAGIC CARROUSEL

**Description:** Larger and more vigorous than most of the miniatures. This is an upright grower which may become rather bare at the base, so prune to prevent legginess. The double flowers which are produced in abundance throughout the season are double and slightly scented. Take half-ripe cuttings in midsummer and insert in sandy compost.

**Special uses:** Suitable for exhibition. Unlike most miniatures, 'Magic Carrousel' is good for cutting.

**Country of origin:** U.S.A.
**Date:** 1972
**Raised by:** Moore
**Type:** Miniature
**Colour:** White, edged with deep pink
**Height:** Approximately 38cm (15in)

# STARINA

**Country of origin:** France
**Date:** 1965
**Raised by:** Meilland
**Type:** Miniature
**Colour:** Orange-red
**Height:** 30cm (1ft) or more

**Description:** Certainly one of the most popular of the miniature roses. It forms a bushy plant with attractive glossy foliage and well-formed flowers produced in abundance. Petals are paler, and are almost gold on the reverse. The brilliance of the flower colour hardly fades with age. This miniature rose can easily be raised from half-ripe cuttings taken in midsummer, and this is well worth doing as this rose is generally not long lived.
**Special uses:** One of the best miniatures for exhibition.

**Description:** An extremely vigorous rambler covered in thorns. It is smothered in fragrant, almost double flowers in early to midsummer. These are coppery pink in bud becoming light pink on opening. Its foliage is a good dark green and glossy and attractive in its own right. A reliable and, on the whole, healthy rose which may be troubled by mildew. Prune out all old stems after flowering and do not be afraid to cut back vigorous growths as this rose could well get out of hand. Despite the fact that it has only one flush of flowers, it is still the best-loved rambler.

**Special uses:** Train its long arching branches to cover a large area of trellis or fence, or over an arch, or into a tree's branches.

**Country of origin:** France
**Date:** 1921
**Raised by:** Barbier
**Type:** Rambler
**Colour:** Pink
**Height:** 6m (20ft) or more

# CRIMSON SHOWER

**Synonym:** 'Red Dorothy Perkins'
**Country of origin:** England
**Date:** 1951
**Raised by:** Norman
**Type:** Rambler
**Colour:** Deep crimson
**Height:** 3m (10ft) or more

**Description:** Very lax habit, with small glossy leaflets, it bears clusters of small double flowers late in summer. Their colour is a wonderful rich glowing crimson, but unfortunately they have no scent. After flowering is over, prune out all the old stems to just above soil level. This will encourage new stems to form which will carry flowers in the coming year.

**Special uses:** With its small flowers and trailing stems, it is at its best trained over an archway, or over a tripod or up a pillar in the border. It also forms a charming weeping standard.

# DORTMUND

**Description:** Strong, vigorous and hardy, this rose is free flowering and recurrent. Its handsome foliage is glossy and dark green. The large single flowers are dark red with white at the centre surrounding yellow stamens.

**Special uses:** Like its stablemate 'Kassel', it may be grown as a shrub or trained up a pillar as it is easy to keep under control. It is suitable for growing against a north-facing wall.

**Country of origin:** Germany
**Date:** 1955
**Raised by:** Kordes
**Type:** Climber
**Colour:** Red and white
**Height:** Approximately 4m (13ft)

# EMILY GRAY

**Country of origin:** England
**Date:** 1918
**Raised by:** Williams
**Type:** Climber
**Colour:** Buff yellow
**Height:** Up to 3m (10ft)

**Description:** Still a favourite despite the fact it only has one flush of flowers early in the summer. However, this is more than made up for by the fine foliage, reddish bronze when young, and the fragrant, semi-double flowers of fine form in a most delightful warm shade of yellow. It is a vigorous and healthy grower. However in exposed areas it is best planted in a protected position as it can show signs of tenderness. Take care not to prune too heavily as new shoots are not readily produced.
**Special uses:** 'Emily Gray' is best when planted against a sheltered south- or west-facing wall.

**Description:** Regarded as the best of all climbing roses. Free flowering and recurrent, the shapely buds open to reveal the outstanding flowers so delicately edged with pink. The foliage is good with a coppery tinge in the dark green. Although this rose stands up well to wet weather, black spot may prove troublesome. It is barely scented.

**Special uses:** An excellent climbing rose for fence, trellis or covering a pergola or an arch.

**Country of origin:** Ireland
**Date:** 1965
**Raised by:** McGredy
**Type:** Climber
**Colour:** Cream flushed with pink
**Height:** Approximately 3m (10ft)

# SCHOOLGIRL

**Country of origin:** Ireland
**Date:** 1964
**Raised by:** McGredy
**Type:** Climber
**Colour:** Apricot
**Height:** Approximately 3m (10ft)

**Description:** The double flowers are recurrent and well formed. Apricot is an unusual colour amongst climbing roses and, although it may fade, the flowers are always lovely. The dark green foliage is somewhat sparse. Although fairly vigorous, the plant soon becomes leggy. It is advisable to prune regularly in order to counteract this unfortunate characteristic. Otherwise plant this climber at the back of the border where its lower regions can be concealed by other plants. Disease resistant.
**Special features:** Fine flowers in form and colour.

# ZEPHIRINE DROUHIN

**Description:** A long-standing favourite. Delightful semi-double flowers, sweetly fragrant, that are produced throughout the summer if dead heads are removed regularly. Known as the thornless rose, this is one of the best loved of the old bourbon roses. Its young foliage is bronze, turning to a good mid-green as it matures. Unfortunately 'Zéphirine Drouhin' is prone to attacks of mildew and black spot, so take routine precautions.

**Special uses:** Grow as a climber or a shrub. It tolerates hard pruning, so can be clipped to form a decorative hedge. Superb over an archway or against trellis. This is one of the few roses suitable for growing against a north-facing wall.

**Country of origin:** France
**Date:** 1868
**Raised by:** Bizot
**Type:** Climber
**Colour:** Deep pink
**Height:** Approximately 3m (10ft)

# FRED LOADS

**Country of origin:** England
**Date:** 1967
**Raised by:** Holmes
**Type:** Modern shrub rose
**Colour:** Vermilion
**Height:** 2.5m (8ft) or more

**Description:** A vigorous and upright growing shrub rose with many very large, semi-double flowers held in large clusters. These are fragrant and recurrent, with the first flush in midsummer. The colour is an attractive soft shade of vermilion. Good resistance to disease and tolerant of wet weather. Do not be afraid to prune this one hard to keep it within bounds.
**Special uses:** One of the best modern shrub roses. It is good for exhibition, and excellent for cutting.

**Description:** Long pointed buds open to reveal large single flowers. These are almost golden yellow towards the centre surrounding a clump of golden stamens. Fragrant and recurrent, the blooms are produced throughout the summer. The foliage is a pale but bright green. A well shaped shrub spreading to 1.5m (5ft), it needs its older branches pruned out and a light trimming back in winter to keep it neat. Orange hips are produced in the autumn; however these are not particularly showy. Good resistance to disease.

**Special uses:** It looks good in a mixed border, and is a lovely specimen shrub.

**Country of origin:** U.S.A.
**Date:** 1956
**Raised by:** Shepherd
**Type:** Modern shrub rose
**Colour:** Primrose yellow
**Height:** Approximately 1.5m (5ft)

# KASSEL

**Country of origin:** Germany
**Date:** 1958
**Raised by:** Kordes
**Type:** Modern shrub rose
**Colour:** Scarlet
**Height:** 1.8m (6ft) or more

**Description:** Glossy dark green foliage sets off the brilliant semi-double flowers to perfection. These are fragrant, of good shape and carried in clusters. Recurrent, with the main flush of flowers in midsummer. A very hardy and vigorous shrub, which can measure up to 1.5m (5ft) across.
**Special uses:** Excellent for training up a pillar as it is often classed as a climbing rose. It tolerates heavy pruning so is a good subject for a hedge.

# MADAME PIERRE OGER

**Description:** This shrub has a slender and upright habit. It is not vigorous and rarely reaches more than 1m (3ft 3in) across. The flowers are most beautiful; cup-shaped and full of petals. Recurrent and richly perfumed, the first of these delicate blooms appear early in summer. Plant in a sunny position to encourage the colour to develop. Black spot is often a problem and routine preventive spraying is almost a necessity.

**Special uses:** The exquisite flowers hold a very special charm. Train over a pillar or tripod in a summer border so that they can be fully appreciated.

**Country of origin:** France
**Date:** 1878
**Raised by:** Oger
**Type:** Old shrub rose (bourbon)
**Colour:** Silvery pink
**Height:** Approximately 1.2m (4ft)

# PENELOPE

**Country of origin:** England
**Date:** 1924
**Raised by:** Pemberton
**Type:** Modern shrub (hybrid musk)
**Colour:** Pale apricot-pink
**Height:** 1.5m (5ft) or more

**Description:** This has long been judged to be one of the best and most reliable of the shrub roses. It has good green foliage, dense vigorous growth and a spreading habit. The flowers are abundant, held in clusters and their colour fades to an attractive creamy pink with age. A healthy rose with a strong musky fragrance. Flowers are produced early in summer and continue into the autumn when small pinkish hips are produced if deadheading has not been too thorough.

**Special uses:** Its dense growth makes it perfect for hedging. A splendid rose for the mixed border. It can also be hard pruned to form a bush if so desired.

**Description:** Spreading to 1.2m (4ft) or more, the arching branches produce single flowers of a most outstanding combination of colours. Occasionally pure yellow flowers occur similar to those of the parent species, *R. foetida*. Long grown in Arab countries, this old shrub rose still has a place in gardens despite its proneness to disease, particularly to black spot. Its introduction to Europe came via Austria, hence its popular name, and many are still found there growing wild. Many modern hybrids owe their colour, lack of scent and susceptibility to black spot to this rose or its parent.

**Special uses:** Outstanding in any border.

**Synonym:** *R. eglanteria* var. *punicea*
**Country of origin:** Unknown, probably Asia Minor
**Introduced:** before 1590, probably from Turkey
**Type:** Old shrub rose
**Colour:** Copper-red with yellow reverse
**Height:** 1.5m (5ft) or more

# ROSA MUNDI  *Rosa gallica* 'Versicolor'

**Country of origin:** Unknown
**Introduced:** before 1665
**Type:** Old shrub rose (gallica)
**Colour:** Crimson splashed and striped with white
**Height:** 1–1.2m (3–4ft)

**Description:** Forms a neat and compact shrub with stems relatively free of thorns. The eye-catching semi-double flowers are produced abundantly in midsummer on previous years' stems. Occasionally some flowers may be pure crimson like the species (the apothecary's rose, *R. gallica*), but all open flat to display the mass of golden stamens. Mildew may be a problem when flowering is over. It owes its familiar name to Fair Rosamond, the mistress of Henry II, with whom the rose has a legendary association.

**Special uses:** A versatile rose which can be grown in a mixed border, planted closely and clipped to form a good hedge.